THE ANCIENT EGYPTIANS

By Jessica Cohn

Gareth Stevens
Publishing

Please visit our website, www.garethstevens.com. For a free color catalog of all our high-quality books, call toll free 1-800-542-2595 or fax 1-877-542-2596.

Library of Congress Cataloging-in-Publication Data
Cohn, Jessica.
The ancient Egyptians / Jessica Cohn.
    p. cm.   (Crafts from the past)
Includes index.
ISBN 978-1-4339-7702-2 (pbk.)
ISBN 978-1-4339-7703-9 (6-pack)
ISBN 978-1-4339-7701-5 (library binding)
1. Egypt Civilization To 332 B.C. Juvenile literature. 2. Egypt Antiquities Juvenile literature.
3. Handicraft Juvenile literature. I. Title. II. Series: Crafts from the past.
DT61.C553 2013
932.01dc23

2012002064

First Edition
Published in 2013 by
Gareth Stevens Publishing
111 East 14th Street, Suite 349
New York, NY 10003

© 2013 Gareth Stevens Publishing

Produced by Netscribes Inc.
Art Director Dibakar Acharjee
Editorial Content The Wordbench
Copy Editor Sarah Chassé
Picture Researcher Sandeep Kumar G

Designer Ravinder Kumar
Illustrators Ashish Tanwar, Indranil Ganguly,
                Prithwiraj Samat and Rohit Sharma

Photo credits:

t = top, a = above, b = below, l = left, r = right, c = center

Front Cover: Netscribes Inc., Shutterstock Images LLC

Title Page: Shutterstock Images LLC

Contents Page: Netscribes Inc.

Netscribes Inc.: 4, 5b, 6, 7t, 7tr, 7bl, 7br, 9t, 9b, 11t, 11cl, 11cr, 11bl, 11br, 15t, 15cl, 15cr, 15b, 17t, 19t, 19cl, 19cr, 19bl, 19br, 20, 23t, 23cl, 23cr, 23bl, 23br, 27tl, 27tr, 27bl, 27br, 28, 21t, 31cl, 32cr, 31bl, 31br, 35tl, 35tr, 35bl, 35br, 38, 39tl, 39tr, 39bl, 39br, 43t, 43cl, 43cl, 43cr, 43bl, 43br

Shutterstock Images LLC: 5t, 8, 10, 13t, 13b, 14, 16t, 16b, 17c, 17b, 18t, 18b, 21, 22, 24, 25t, 25b, 26t, 26b, 29t: Vladimir Korostyshevskiy, 29b, 30c, 30b, 32cl, 32cr, 32b, 33: Jose Gil, 34, 36, 37t, 37b, 40, 41t, 41b, 45br, 48b

IstockPhoto: 12

NASA, ESA, and A. Aloisi (Space Telescope Science Institute and European Space Agency, Baltimore, Md.): 42b

Printed in the United States of America

CPSIA compliance information: Batch #CS12GS: For further information contact Gareth Stevens, New York, New York at 1-800-542-2595.

Contents

River of Life

The Nile is a river more than 4,000 miles long, bringing life to the desert around it. Every year, the river floods its banks in Egypt. Then the waters recede and leave behind soil that is good for farming. The ancient Egyptians built their entire society on the rich soil of the **floodplain** along the Nile's banks.

Heart of Egypt

Near the Mediterranean Sea, the water slows down, and the Nile fans out. The slower water leaves behind dirt and rocks. These have built up over time to create a triangle of land called a **delta**. The ancient Egyptians built their capital at the southern edge of the delta. Their great city was known as Memphis.

Nefertiti was an Egyptian queen who lived from about 1370 B.C. to 1330 B.C.

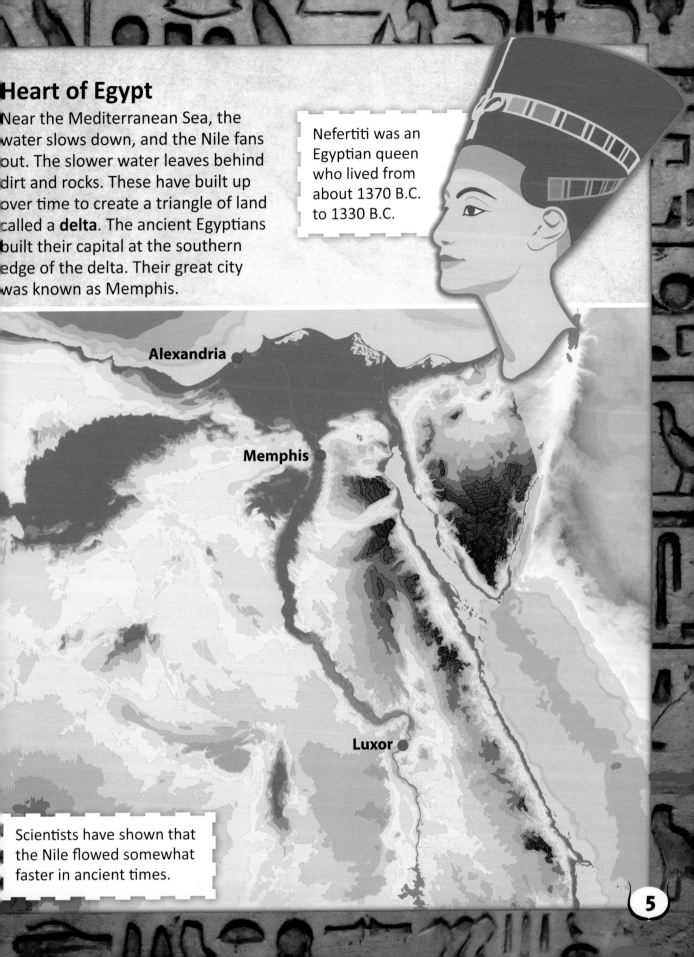

Alexandria

Memphis

Luxor

Scientists have shown that the Nile flowed somewhat faster in ancient times.

Egyptians had barges for moving everything from food supplies to giant stone statues. The rulers had special barges on which they could relax and have parties.

Living on the Water

The Nile was the main way of moving goods and people from place to place. The water flows from south to north. By following the flow, it was easy enough to move full boats north. This is why most of the cities grew in the delta in the north. To travel south, the Egyptians powered their boats with sails or huge teams of **oarsmen**.

Close-Up

The shape of the Nile and its delta reminded ancient Egyptians of a local flower called the **lotus**. Lotus flowers grow along the Nile. They close every night and bloom every morning. Egyptians saw this as a symbol of rebirth and the power of the sun. Lotus flowers became common in Egyptian art and myths.

Reed Boat

Wood was rare, as trees were hard to come by in the desert, so most Egyptian boats were made of reeds, which grew in the delta. To see how, try making your own boat to sail in a sink.

Materials Needed
- Raffia "grass" from a craft store
- Scissors
- Tape
- Small rubber bands

1 Get about 20 pieces of raffia together and cut them so they are 9 or so inches long. Then tape or band them together in the middle to create a bundle.

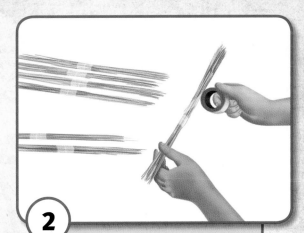

2 Repeat Step 1 again until you have seven or so bundles of equal length.

3 Lay the bundles side by side on a table. Run a piece of tape loosely around the middle of all the bundles to stick them together.

4 Now, band all of the bundles together as tightly as you can on each end. This should make your boat a banana shape. Put it in water and see how it floats.

Source of Riches

The ancient Egyptians made the most of the natural resources in and around the river. The Nile was full of fish for food. **Papyrus** plants were plentiful along the water. The stems were turned into paper and woven into baskets and other items. The land was covered with rock formations, and the people became experts at mining for stone. They also mined metals, such as copper, and precious stones, such as emeralds.

The Lower Nile, in the north, was where most people lived. The Upper Nile, in the south, was full of farms, villages, and pits for digging stone.

Black and Red

Egyptians talked about their land in terms of two areas. The land near the Nile was rich and black in color, so they called it the black land. Away from the river, Egypt was full of rocky deserts and mountains. This was the red land. Besides being full of stone and metals, the red land was hard to cross. It protected Egypt from invaders.

The mushroom rocks in the Egyptian desert were shaped by blowing sand over a long, long time.

All That Glitters

Egyptians valued gold, as most ancient people did. However, early Egyptians may have prized silver even more. Egypt had many gold mines. On the other hand, silver was rare and had to be **imported**. Because of this, only the **pharaohs** and other rich Egyptians could afford silver jewelry and treasures.

Gold was associated with the skin of the gods, but silver was said to be the bones of the gods.

Close-Up

Scarabs were special charms carved in the image of the scarab beetle. Egyptians worshipped the beetles because baby scarabs would show up as if they came out of thin air. The charms were often made of common stones, though some were made of metal and set with rubies and other jewels. The charms were thought to bring luck. They often carried religious sayings and well wishes.

Scarabs differ around the world. The kind that was considered special in ancient Egypt has six rays around the head.

Quite Charming

Do you need a bit of ancient Egyptian luck? You can make your own scarab charm necklace very easily.

Materials Needed
- Self-drying clay
- Toothpick
- Chenille stem or pipe cleaner
- Scissors
- Yarn

1 Shape a piece of clay into the body. Use the toothpick to carve the wings and head.

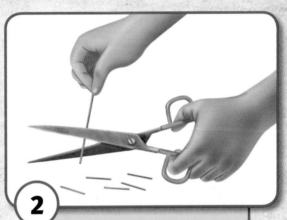

2 Cut the chenille stem in six pieces. Attach them where the legs belong.

3 Poke a hole at one end of the body, big enough to fit the yarn. Let the clay dry overnight.

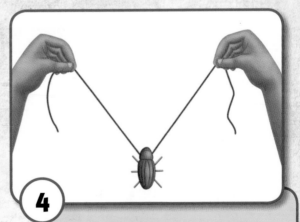

4 Now, string some yarn through the hole and tie the ends together to complete your necklace.

Feeling Classy

In Egypt, a person's class was based on the job he or she did. Most Egyptians were farmers or captured slaves. The farmers were bound to the land they worked. The slaves were bonded to families in the higher classes. Free craftsmen were in a class above farmers. Then came soldiers and scribes. Scribes were the only people who could read and write. It was their job to keep records.

It was nearly impossible, in ancient Egypt, to change rank.

Pharaoh

Priests and nobles

Traders, artisans, shopkeepers, and scribes

Farmers and herders

Unskilled workers

Power in Place

Nobles and priests had power over their regions and temples. They worked to keep the people and the gods happy. At the very top, the pharaoh was in charge of the entire empire. He or she was considered a god on Earth. The pharaoh had a chief adviser called a **vizier**, who handled government work. This official was sometimes a high priest.

Pharaohs showed off their power by building huge statues of themselves, such as this one of Ramses II at Abu Simbel. It is over 60 feet tall.

Animal Kingdom

Egyptians saw the animals around them as symbols of life forces and even as gods. **Jackals** were wild dogs that stood for death and judgment in the afterlife. Cats were popular pets that were said to stand for **grace**. Crocodiles were common in the Nile. They were said to show the pharaoh's strength. Hippos meant rebirth and fertility.

Anubis, god of the afterlife, was shown as a jackal with a crown or as a man with a jackal's head.

Close-Up

In Egypt, cows were valuable, and they were carefully guarded. Every other year, the Egyptians held a cattle **census**. Every cow in Egypt had to be counted and recorded. This may sound like a dirty job, but it was very important. In fact, the count was so important that the vizier ran it himself.

Cattle Call

It's easy to make your own cow. Just remember to register it with the vizier, or he might tell the pharaoh on you.

Materials Needed
- Jar with a lid
- Masking tape
- Two toilet paper tubes
- Cardboard scraps
- Glue
- Paint, including pink for the nose
- Markers

1 Make sure the lid is tight on the jar. Then cover the jar, but not the lid, completely with masking tape.

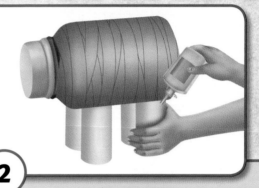

2 Cut your paper tubes in half and tape or glue them in pairs on each end of the jar. These will be the legs. You can stand the jar on its side now.

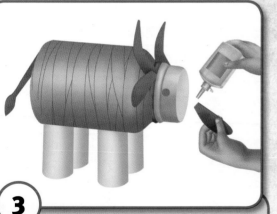

3 Cut out ears, eyes, and horns from the cardboard. The lid will be the nose. Glue or tape the other details in place above it. You can also add a tail.

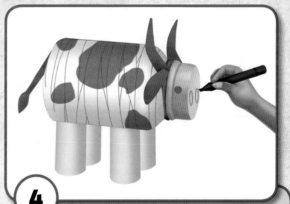

4 Paint the lid pink and the rest cow colors. Use the marker to draw nostrils on the lid. Add spots or fantastic details if you like.

From the Gods

According to the ancient Egyptian religion, the gods had power over nature and life events such as childbirth and marriage. Yet the gods shared part of their creative power with each person. This power was in the **ka**. The ka was a person's life force, or "spiritual double." It guided him or her to lead a good life.

At the tomb of Tutankhamen, there are two statues that stand guard over him. They look very similar. They are said to represent the king and his ka.

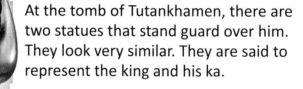

True to Your Ka

The ka was also like a conscience. When people did bad deeds, they were thought to be neglecting their ka. People made special offerings of food and drink to their own ka to keep them strong. The ka also lived on after a person's death as long as his or her body stayed intact. This is why Egyptians **mummified** their dead.

Egyptians used a ritual process to wrap and preserve the bodies of important people after death.

Dying in Style

Egyptians believed that a person who died went on living. To Egyptians, the afterlife meant living among the gods in a heavenly version of Egypt. Egyptians often buried their dead with treasures and tools for use in the afterlife.

For some pharaohs and nobles, burial was a last chance to show off. They had fancy gold death masks and were buried in tombs surrounded by treasure.

Close-Up

One of the most famous Egyptian texts is *The Book of the Dead*. It was not a single book. It was a series of stories and bits of advice. Copies of these stories were often placed in Egyptian tombs and sometimes carved into their walls. The texts included important information, such as descriptions of gods and tips on how to navigate the afterlife.

It was said that the god Anubis weighed a dead person's heart against a feather to see if it had become heavy from evil deeds. If a person's heart was light, he or she got to enjoy the afterlife.

Facing Death

The pharaohs used to cover their burial masks with gold. Now, you can make a mask of your own. However, you may want to use less expensive materials.

Materials Needed
- Costume mask, such as an alien face
- Pencil
- Poster board
- Scissors
- Tape
- Paint and markers
- Paintbrush

1 Place the mask on the board. Outline the mask, then draw a "headdress" around it.

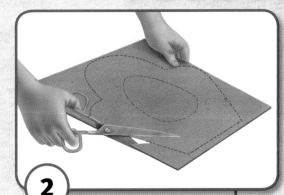

2 Cut off the extra board. Then cut out the mask outline to make a hole.

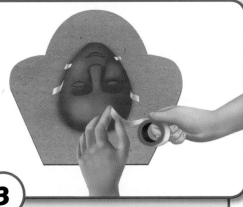

3 Punch the mask through the hole, and tape the mask in place on both sides.

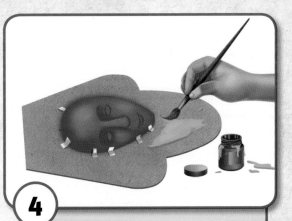

4 Paint over the mask, tape, and headdress in one color, such as yellow. Then decorate the face and headdress.

The construction projects completed by the ancient Egyptians amaze today's engineers. The Egyptians were good at working with stone. They were great builders. The most famous type of building they made is the **pyramid**. The Egyptians built pyramids as tombs for the pharaohs. These huge structures had a square base and four triangles for the sides.

The Great Pyramid at Giza was built for a pharaoh named Khufu. It is the largest of three pyramids at the same site. At nearly 481 feet high, it was the world's tallest building from 2550 B.C. until nearly 4,000 years later.

Beyond the Pyramids

The Egyptians built monuments and temples of distinctive shapes and sizes. They also built tall stone statues to honor the gods. One of the more interesting shapes in use was the **obelisk**. This was a tall pillar with a square base, steeply sloping sides, and a small pyramid on top.

Obelisks were found all over Egypt. They had prayers and stories written on them.

The Sphinx is a huge statue of a lion with a man's head. It was built right next to the Great Pyramid. Its nose fell off many years ago.

21

Brick Houses

When building houses, regular Egyptians used what they had around them. They used the sun to dry mud from the river into bricks. They used dry reeds and straw to make roofs. The homes of the poor had only one or two rooms. The richest people had large mansions made of stone. Some even had swimming pools.

Close-Up

Because wood was scarce, most Egyptian homes had little furniture beyond the essentials. There were oil lamps for lighting at night. Reed baskets and pottery were common. Wood and leather bed frames, small tables, and stools could be found in many homes. Full armchairs were a luxury for only the wealthiest.

Mud bricks were easy to make, but they also fell apart quickly. The Egyptians had to work just to keep their houses up.

Pyramid Scheme

The Great Pyramid is so well built that no two sides are more than 8 inches different in length. Can you do as well when you make your own pyramid from cardboard and sand?

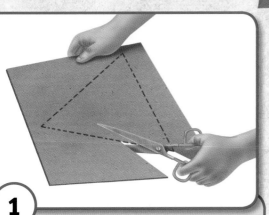

1 Cut a square of cardboard and measure the length of the sides. Using the same length, cut out four triangles with equal sides.

2 Glue and tape the bottom of each triangle to each side of the square firmly. Then, one by one, tape the triangles together so that they meet at the top. Tape any loose parts.

3 Cover the pyramid with one or two layers of glue. Place the pyramid inside a container for this step, or it could get messy.

4 Pour the sand or brown sugar over the pyramid until it is covered. Let the glue dry, then remove your pyramid for show.

Turning the Desert Green

The flooding of the Nile covered the ground with **alluvial** soil. This soil had rich nutrients right on top, so it was easy to grow plants in it. The farmers' biggest challenge was making sure the water reached the far ends of the fields. They used canals and **levees** to steer the water to their crops.

To control water in ancient Egypt, levees were built up along more than 600 miles of one bank of the Nile.

Know to Grow

The main crops were grains such as barley and wheat. Because Egypt relied on the flood, it had only one farming season. This meant everything was harvested at once. The Egyptians then stored the grain in **granaries** to last until the next harvest. The Egyptians were also expert beekeepers. Honey was one of their favorite treats.

Records of beekeeping date to 2400 B.C., making Egyptians some of the first people to keep bees for honey.

In one season, Egyptians produced and stored enough grain to feed everyone and even sell the extra to other countries.

Food on the Table

Compared with other ancient people, the Egyptians ate well. The people baked and ate bread and brewed and drank beer. Even poor Egyptians could enjoy a wide variety of vegetables and beans that grew by the Nile. Egyptian towns also had butcher shops, where people could purchase fresh meat.

Close-Up

Few specifics are known about Egyptian recipes, but it is clear Egyptians cooked a lot. It seems that most people ate ducks, geese, and other poultry, but the rich had a wider variety of meat. The Egyptians baked, boiled, fried, grilled, and roasted their food. They had spices, including mustard, for flavor.

The ancient Egyptians used dates as a sweetener.

Today, wheat is used to make bread that is soft. In ancient Egypt, wheat bread was hard on the teeth.

Go Bowling

Follow these steps to make a footed bowl. In tombs in Egypt, bowls with feet held water, a symbol of life.

Materials Needed
- Ball of self-drying clay
- Two smaller pieces of clay

1 First, shape the ball of clay into a small bowl. Take your thumb and press it firmly in the ball's center so that the inside of the bowl begins to take shape.

2 Pinch the ends of the clay that are sticking out. Shape the rim of the bowl.

3 Once the bowl is complete, take the two smaller pieces of clay and begin to roll them into short, fat cylinders. These will be the feet.

4 Bend the middle of each cylinder at a right angle. Attach one end to the bottom of the bowl. Pinch the other into feet until the bowl stands.

Dressed Like an Egyptian

Egyptian clothing was simple and practical. Because Egypt was warm year-round, almost all clothing was made of light linen and designed to keep its wearer cool. Men wore a simple wrap around the waist. Women wore linen dresses with shoulder straps. Most people walked around barefoot, but they had sandals for special occasions.

Despite what modern costumes of ancient Egypt show, most clothes were not dyed or decorated.

Fresh and Clean

Cleanliness was very important to Egyptians. They did not have soap until later in their history, so keeping clothes clean was a tough job early on. Rich people had their linens cleaned with lye at washhouses. Poor people braved crocodile attacks to wash in the river. As for the pharaoh, there were multiple officials whose only job was to keep the pharaoh's clothes clean.

Priests dressed up, wearing animal skins and ceremonial headdresses.

Painted Faces

In Egypt, both men and women used makeup and cosmetics. Some of this was practical. Oil was used to protect skin from sunburn or from drying out in the desert air. Both men and women wore distinctive black eye makeup called **kohl**. They also used perfumes made of flowers, fruits, and spices such as cinnamon.

Close-Up

Kohl was especially important to ancient Egyptians. Not only was eye makeup considered attractive, it also had religious functions. The eye was shaped into an almond shape, as seen on Egyptian gods. Doctors prescribed kohl to treat eye ailments. Even newborn babies were painted with kohl—to protect them from curses.

People have fanciful ideas about the Egyptians as seen in computer-made art. Some of what is shown here is correct. In addition to kohl, Egyptians also wore rouge to redden their cheeks. They dyed their lips, hair, and fingernails with henna. However, the best way to study what they looked like is to look at ancient art.

By the Collar

The collar necklace, or **usekh**, is a fashion item for men and women that started in ancient Egypt and still exists today. Try making your own. It may not be gold like the pharaoh's, but it will be unique.

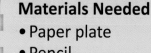

Materials Needed
- Paper plate
- Pencil
- Scissors
- Colored pencils and paint
- Paintbrush
- Optional: Adult to help with step 2

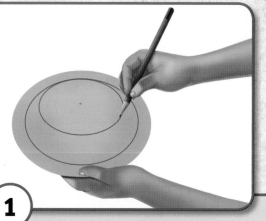

1

Mark a spot on the back of the paper plate about an inch from the edge. Starting at that point, trace a circle on the back of the plate that is big enough for your neck.

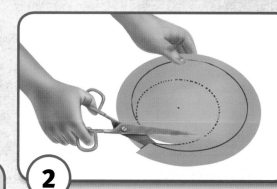

2

Cut from the edge of the plate to the spot. Then, cut out the circle. Make sure the plate fits your neck comfortably; adjust as needed.

3

Draw layers of circles around the neck hole. Color them in contrasting colors.

4

Use the paint to add "jewels." Dab the paint on to make dots.

Art for Life

As in other ancient cultures, art in Egypt both honored the gods and royalty and showed scenes from everyday life. The Egyptians made statues, pottery, and jewelry. Their art pieces often featured special symbols. Some of the symbols, such as the **Eye of Horus**, honored the gods. Others were charms, such as the **ankh** sign, which meant "life."

The ankh (at left) was also called the key of the Nile or the key of life.

The Eye of Horus had six parts that represented touch, taste, hearing, sight, smell, and thought.

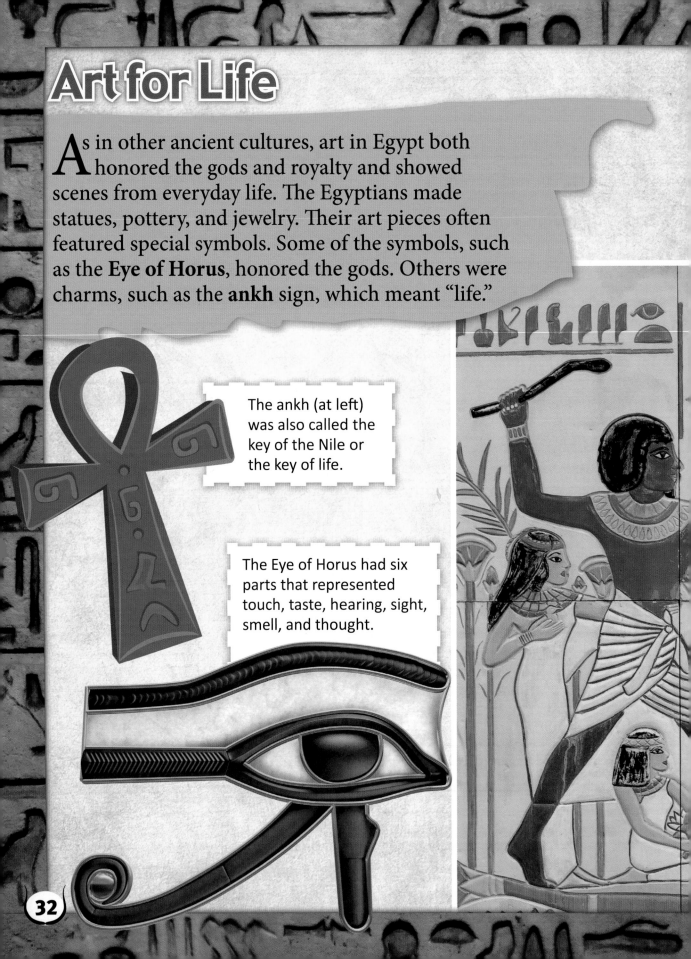

Lack of Perspective

One of the first things people notice about Egyptian paintings is their flat style. This is because their artists did not know how to use **perspective** to make their pictures show depth. Instead, Egyptian art often shows people from the side on a flat background, much like a cartoon. The artists wanted to show ideas rather than be realistic.

Egyptian paintings were sometimes done on papyrus and parchment, but most of the ones that survive today were painted on stone walls.

33

Musical Land

Men and women could work as musicians in ancient Egypt. They performed at parties and festivals. At times, they were told to entertain the pharaoh. The Egyptian musicians played all sorts of instruments. They had harps, flutes, and all kinds of drums. Singers and dancers were a part of the performances as well.

Close-Up

Each temple hired a special musician to play at ceremonies. This job was considered a high honor. A rattle called a **sistrum** was the key sound in religious music. Other instruments were sometimes playing as well, along with singing or chanting.

Most of the instruments with strings were played with bows, but lutes were plucked with the fingers.

It is hard to know exactly what Egyptian music sounded like, because the Egyptians did not write their music down.

Get Rattled

If you want to entertain yourself like the Egyptians would, you can start by crafting an instrument that makes a rattling sound much like a sistrum would.

1 Close and tape one end of the tube.

2 Add metal objects inside until it makes a strong sound when shaken. If there are too many or too few objects, the rattle will be too quiet.

3 Twist the other end shut. Wrap tightly with tape for a handle.

4 Decorate as desired, perhaps with an Eye of Horus, an ankh sign, or your initials.

In the Ballpark

Egyptian children were encouraged to exercise at an early age. Children mostly played ball games that were much like handball and field hockey. They wrestled and ran races. As they grew up, the best athletes could compete at festivals. Even the pharaohs enjoyed watching sporting events.

The Egyptians also had games that were much like soccer and bowling.

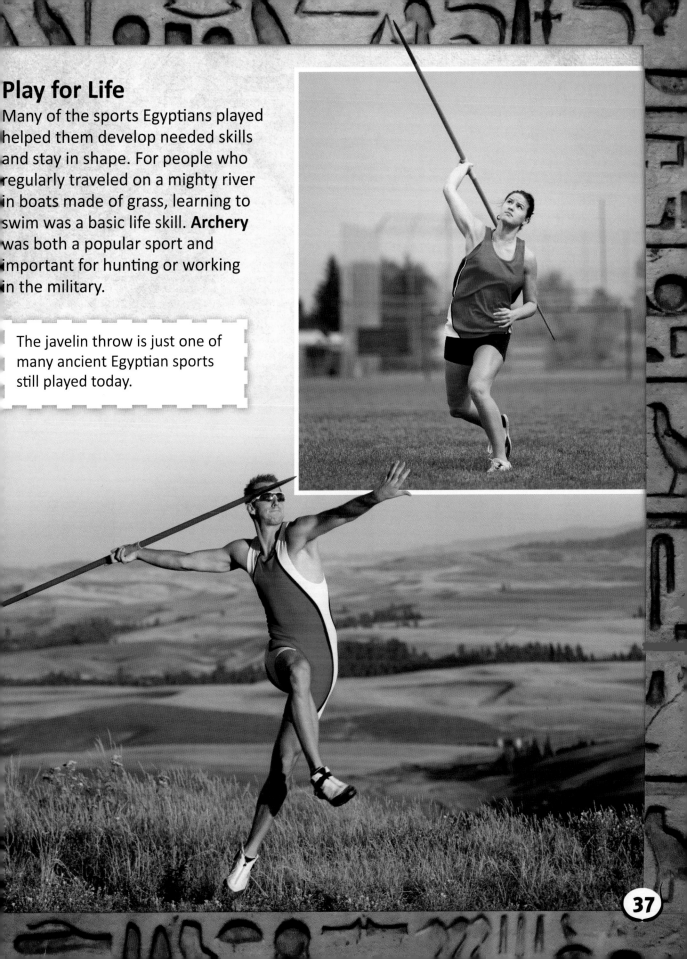

Play for Life

Many of the sports Egyptians played helped them develop needed skills and stay in shape. For people who regularly traveled on a mighty river in boats made of grass, learning to swim was a basic life skill. **Archery** was both a popular sport and important for hunting or working in the military.

The javelin throw is just one of many ancient Egyptian sports still played today.

Game Night

In addition to sports, many Egyptians enjoyed games of strategy. They played a number of popular board games. The rules to most of these games have been lost. However, it is clear that Egyptians made board games out of clay. They moved their pieces using counting sticks or six-sided number cubes.

Close-Up

One of the ancient games with known rules was **senet**. Senet was played by two players. The object was to move five to seven pieces along the board in an S shape. The player who moved all of his or her pieces to the last square first won.

Senet was played on a board with 30 squares. The game had some sort of religious purpose. Some ancient texts describe the gods playing the game.

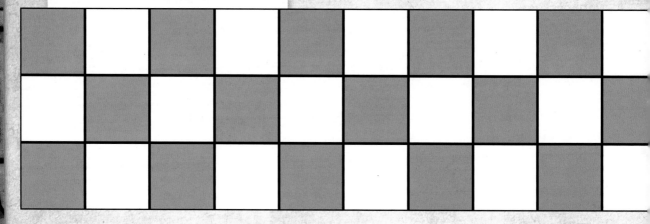

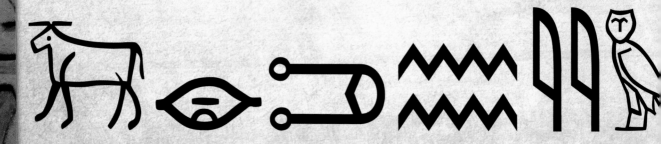

Like a Snake

Mehen was played on a board that looked like a coiled snake. Though we do not know the rules, you can try rolling a die to move playing pieces along. Race to the center!

Materials Needed

- Die, or self-drying clay and pencil
- Large colored paper
- Marker
- Ruler
- Coins, stones, or beans for markers

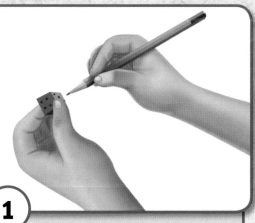

1 Get a die or make one from self-drying clay. Use a pencil to poke one through six dots, so each side is different.

2 While the cube dries, trace a circle on the colored paper and cut it out. This will be the playing board.

3 With a marker, create a swirl pattern on the paper that ends in the center. In between each line of the swirl, use a ruler to make evenly spaced boxes.

4 To make a more authentic board, decorate the middle so that the boxes end in a snake's head. Roll and play!

Taught at Home

Even though they had few formal schools, Egyptian children were always learning. Girls of all classes learned cooking and housekeeping from their mothers. Most boys learned trade skills from their fathers. A few boys, who were set to be scribes or artists, went to school to learn reading and writing.

Boys studied to be scribes by copying existing texts.

Family Business

For the most part, Egyptian children had to learn and eventually take over their parents' jobs. Children of basket weavers would grow up to be basket weavers, too. This was not true just for boys. Compared with other ancient cultures, Egypt had fewer rules against girls learning a trade and working. There were even a few female pharaohs.

Cleopatra became the pharaoh in about 51 B.C. She was the last female pharaoh.

Place Yourself in Egypt

Which job would you enjoy?

Written in Stone

How does anyone know anything about a culture that began over 5,000 years ago? It is not easy. The Egyptians wrote things down, but there was a problem. Most of the writing used a complicated writing system called **hieroglyphics**. Up until the early 1800s, nobody knew how to read it.

Close-Up

In 1799, French soldiers found the Rosetta stone. It has a message carved on it in three writing styles. One is hieroglyphics. Another is demotic, which was a common way to write Egyptian. The third is Greek. Experts knew how to read two of the three. By comparing the messages, a man named Jean-François Champollion figured out how to read hieroglyphics.

The name of royalty was placed in a flattened circle with an end line to show its importance. The name of this marking is a **cartouche**. It works like a frame around the name. Why not make the same mark around your own name, using paper and pencil?

This is the cartouche of Ramses the Great, found at Abu Simbel.

Picture This

Try writing your name and age, using the charts. Though the Egyptians wrote from right to left and top to bottom as well, you can write from left to right, in the usual way.

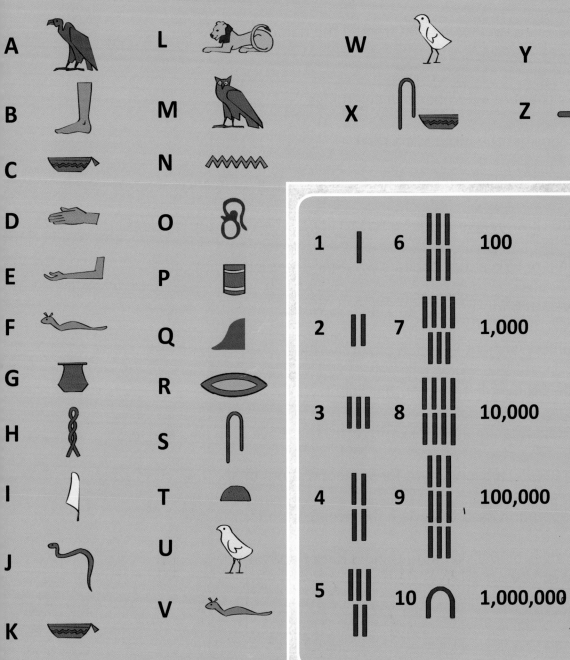

Glossary

alluvial—relating to deposits left at the mouth of a river

ankh—symbol with a cross and a loop; sign that stood for life in ancient Egypt

archery—shooting with a bow and an arrow

cartouche—flat, oval figure that framed the names of rulers on Egyptian monuments

census—a count of a number of living things

delta—deposit at the mouth of a river

Eye of Horus—eyelike symbol of protection and power in ancient Egypt

floodplain—low-lying area that tends to flood when a waterway does

grace—help or virtue that appears whether deserved or not

granaries—storehouses for grains such as wheat

hieroglyphics—ancient Egyptian picture writing

imported—brought in from another country

jackals—doglike animals in Asia and Africa that have long ears and legs

ka—term used in ancient Egypt for someone's soul or spirit

kohl—preparation used to darken the eyelid or under the eye

levees—ridges or walls created to hold back floodwater

lotus—type of water lily

mehen—ancient board game played on a path of squares that coil like a snake

mummified—dried as a mummy, which was a dead body preserved with salts

oarsmen—people who use paddles to power boats through water

obelisk—pillar with four sides and a pyramid at the top

papyrus—type of plant that can be pressed into a kind of paper

perspective—representing depth and distance on a flat surface using lines and shade

pharaohs—rulers of ancient Egypt

pyramid—structure with square base and triangular sides that meet at a point at the top

scarabs—beetles of a certain type

senet—ancient board game with 30 squares

sistrum—ancient musical instrument with rods or loops on a metal frame

usekh—type of necklace

vizier—high-level official in ancient Egypt and elsewhere

For Further Information

Books

Ancient Egypt. Stewart Ross. (Gareth Stevens, 2006)

Eyewitness: Ancient Egypt. George Hart. (DK Publishing, 2000)

National Geographic Kids Everything Ancient Egypt. Crispin Boyer. (National Geographic, 2011)

Websites

Discovering Egypt
http://www.discoveringegypt.com/

Children's author Mark Millmore offers a collection of Egyptian games and interactive lessons, including math worksheets in Egyptian numerals.

Kidipede: Ancient Egypt
http://www.historyforkids.org/learn/egypt/

Who was Isis? How can a soul be weighed? This Kidipede site offers links covering many subjects.

The British Museum: Ancient Egypt
http://www.ancientegypt.co.uk/menu.html

Read about ancient storytelling and much more while exploring the British Museum's online exhibits.

Zahi Hawass
http://www.drhawass.com/blog/kids-tips-budding-archaeologists

Zahi Hawass is the famous archaeologist who explored the tombs of the pyramid's builders. His site for students features maps, diaries, and news about the ancient world.

Index

Things to Think About and Do

Final Word

Egyptian scribes sometimes wrote something called wisdom literature. This was usually written as a set of instructions from a famous father to his son about how to live a good life. But it was actually written to teach the public about morals. Most wisdom literature is short, simple advice that could easily be remembered and recited to those who could not read it themselves. Here's an example from *The Instruction of Ani*:

> *Befriend one who is straight and true*
> *One whose actions you have seen.*
> *If your rightness matches his,*
> *The friendship will be balanced.*

Try It!

Try writing your own instructions. Pick an important lesson that you have learned and try to write it as if you are teaching a friend who does not understand it.